The Apple Farm

Written by Claire Daniel

Illustrated by Bill Farnsworth

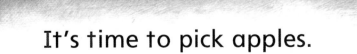

It's time to pick apples.

We pick red apples.

We pick yellow and green apples.

5

Everyone's picking apples.

We need all the apples.

We need the red ones.

We need the yellow and green ones.

Everyone's picking apples.

We need all our apples to make apple pie.

We need all our apples to make applesauce.

Everyone's picking apples.

It's time to go.
Everyone's taking the apples home.

The apples are in boxes.
The apples are in baskets and bags.

The apples look good.

The apples smell good.

This apple is mine.
Yum!
It tastes good.